I0759940

This book is dedicated to all the diplomats who defied official policy to save countless lives during World War II:

Raoul Wallenberg, Chiune Sugihara, Feng Shan Ho, Georg Ferdinand Duckwitz, Carl Lutz, Selahattin Ulkumen, Florian Manoliu, Giorgio Perlasca, Francis Foley, Jose Santaella, Franjo Puncuch, Elow Kihlgren, Angelo Rotta, Constantin Karadja, Jan Zwartendijk, Luis Martins de Souza Dantas, Jean-Edouard Friedrich, Harald Feller, Peter Zurcher, Ernst Vonrufs, Aracy De Carvalho, Ernst Prodolliet, Friedrich Born, Per Anger, Lars Berg, Carl Iva Danielsson, Valdemar Langlet, Angel Sanz-Briz, Abdol-Hossein Sardari, Othon De Bogaerde de Terbrugge, Necdet Kent, Hiram Bingham, Gilberto Bosques, Eduardo Proper de Callejon, Eero Harjanne, Kauko Sipinen, Rudolf Salek, Jose Arturo Castellanos, Giuseppe Agenore Magno, Alberto Carlos de Lis-Teixeira Branquinho, Jules Gulden, Francois Pongracz, Sebastian Romero Radigales, Guelfo Zamboni, and Angelo Guiseppe Roncalli.

~ E. B. and M. C.

Library of Congress Cataloging-in-Publication Data available.

ISBN 978-1-4521-7098-5

Manufactured in China.

Design by Amelia Mack and Jennifer Tolo Pierce.
Typeset in Analogue.
The illustrations in this book were rendered in pencil and digitally colored.

10 9 8 7 6 5 4 3 2 1

Chronicle Books LLC
680 Second Street
San Francisco, California 94107

Chronicle Books—we see things differently. Become part of our community at www.chroniclekids.com.

The World Entire

A True Story of an Extraordinary World War II Rescue

By Elizabeth Brown

Illustrated by Melissa Castrillón

CHRONICLE BOOKS
SAN FRANCISCO

Aristides de Sousa Mendes lived with his wife and their many children in Portugal, where Europe reaches out into the ocean. There, in a little town encircled by sunbaked hills, laughter warmed his family's days as much as the sun. And music lit their nights as much as the moon.

On Thursdays, Aristides opened his kitchen to the children of the town. The town wasn't a wealthy place, but Aristides' door was always open. He baked bread and made soup and served them at his table on chilly days.

Aristides was a diplomat. Though he sometimes lived in other countries, Portugal was his home, and some days he drove from there all the way across the north of Spain to his office in Bordeaux, France. It was his job to review requests from anyone who wanted to enter Portugal from there.

A family going on vacation?

Yes.

A businessman with automobiles to sell in Porto?

Yes.

A French diplomat on his way to see the prime minister in Lisbon?

Yes.

Aristides signed his name and stamped each of their passports.

Ambassadors and even
presidents from other countries
often visited consulates in Portugal.
They danced in suits and gowns
at fancy balls. Their world was
proper, polished, and perfect.

But storm clouds were gathering on Bordeaux's azure horizon, darker than any seen before.

Fighter planes roared overhead.

War was breaking out all over Europe

as German soldiers, Nazis, invaded Poland, Denmark, and Norway, and then Belgium, the Netherlands . . . and France.

Each day they marched closer and closer to Bordeaux.

People from invaded countries also journeyed on the crowded roads toward Bordeaux with all they could carry, frightened of the storm that was coming.

They gathered outside Aristides' office: Mothers, fathers, children. Doctors, inventors, poets.

Families from all over Europe.

They were refugees, driven from their homes, their countries, and everything they ever knew and loved.

They wanted to survive. Spain was sympathetic to the Nazis. Portugal was their last hope.

But over the mountains in Portugal,
the prime minister didn't want
to take care of any refugees.

While Portugal officially took no side in the war, its leaders were not interested in helping the people fleeing the Nazi army. The prime minister had ordered Portugal's diplomats not to give visas to anyone hoping to escape.

Aristides asked
his government permission to
grant visas anyway.

No.

When more families came,
he asked again.

No.

Each day, more and more people,
hundreds at a time, arrived at the grand stone
building by the river, begging for visas.

They waited outside on the street,
down the city block, never leaving their place
in line, fearful of losing their chance.
Again, Aristides asked if he could issue visas.
Again, his government refused.

At night, Aristides was driven
around Bordeaux, stopping here and
there to see the growing numbers of stranded refugees.
He met a rabbi—a refugee himself—who was helping
Jewish families at a local synagogue.

Soon
Aristides and
the rabbi became
the best of friends. The
rabbi explained what would happen
to the refugees if they did not receive visas.
Many would be captured by the Nazis.
They would be sent to camps to be tortured
and killed. Families would be separated,
and children taken away.

Aristides offered the rabbi and his family
visas, but the rabbi shook his head.

"It is not just my family who needs help,"
he said, "but all my fellow Jews who
are in danger for their lives."

Aristides grew sick with worry. For three days, he wrung his hands. He paced his apartment. He heard the rabbi's words echo in his head.

Outside the consulate, more and more families gathered each day.
Panic spread.
Refugees pounded on the door and shouted to the windows.

Help us!

Save us!

We must get to Portugal.

Aristides tossed and turned in his bed. He thought about what it would be like if his family were in the same situation.

How could he live with himself if he didn't help? What if all these children were his own?

On the third day, Aristides gathered his family around him. Together they created a production line inside his office. Then Aristides flung open the doors onto the street.

"From now on, I will give visas to everyone," he announced.

"Next person, please."

Refugees lined up outside the office,
down the stairs,
in the hallway,
and in the dining room,
sleeping on chairs,
the floor,
the rugs,
and the street.

A family of musicians?

Yes.

An engineer?

Yes.

A professor? An artist?

Yes. Yes.

A mother? A carpenter? A child?

Yes, yes, yes.

One girl brought a diamond to Aristides to pay for a visa, telling him that her parents had been killed.

"Quick, hide that in your pocket," Aristides said to the child.

He fed the girl, gave her a visa, and arranged for a group of refugees to take her to safety.

Aristides worked faster and faster. Every second wasted was another visa he could have issued.

As the Nazis got closer,
more families arrived.

Aristides' wife comforted
a mother, helped a crying child,
and offered water to the people
standing in line.

Aristides' sons and nephew
helped him stamp visas.

Aristides signed visa
after visa after visa after visa.
The more ink that flowed from his pen,
the more lives he might be able to save.
He shortened his signature to *Mendes*,
hoping to make the ink last—
long enough to save them all.

Minute after minute,
hour after hour,
family after family,
they pressed on.

Aristides' back ached. His neck and shoulders were stiff. His writing hand cramped. But he had to make visas for all the refugees he could before the Portuguese government sent policemen to stop him.

For five days and four nights they stamped and Aristides signed until no more families climbed up the stairs.

Only one family
remained—
his own.

Aristides hugged them more tightly than ever before and sent his sons and nephew home to Portugal.

The radio announced the news—German troops were only miles from Bordeaux.

Closer to the border,
the Portuguese consulate in Bayonne
was overwhelmed by refugees. Aristides had
authorized the vice-consul there to issuc visas,
but there were too many people, and there
wasn't much time. He told Aristides
that he needed help.

Aristides drove to Bayonne as fast as he could.

The consulate was flooded with people trying to escape to Portugal.

So Aristides quickly set up a table on the street.

He stamped and signed all night long, sure by now that Portuguese police knew what he was doing and would come for him. But he worked until his fingers trembled from exhaustion and until as many people as he could help held a visa in their hand.

When the German army advanced into Bayonne, Aristides turned his car toward Hendaye, at the northernmost border between France and Spain.

There, Spain had sealed the bridge that linked France to Spain, and the Spanish guards refused to let any refugees cross who held visas.

So, Aristides led the families through the hillsides on a quiet back road he had often taken as a shortcut between Portugal and France.

He brought them to a small border crossing hidden in the hills, far enough away that the guards would not yet have received orders to turn away those holding visas signed by him.

"I am the Portuguese consul,"
Aristides shouted.
"These people are with me."

The guards checked
each visa,
one at a time—
each name, each face,
each stamp.
Finally, they waved
the refugees on.

Aristides opened the border fence, and the refugees crossed into Spain.

From there, they would continue on to Portugal, where the sunbaked hills could encircle them, and the ocean waves in Lisbon's harbor could carry them to new countries and new lives. It was time for Aristides to return to Portugal as well.

PORTUGAL

When Aristides reached home, the Portuguese police, who couldn't catch him in France, were waiting.

They led him to jail, charging him with disobedience against his government. Aristides had ten days to prepare to defend himself and wrote: "It was indeed my aim to 'save all those people,' whose suffering was indescribable."

But the court found
Aristides guilty.
His government took
away his job.

He lost his home.

His children were not permitted to go to university or work in Portugal.

Now, his family went to soup kitchens for their supper.

But there, Aristides met his friend the rabbi and his family! And there, too, were others who had escaped.

A builder. Yes.

A baker. Yes.

A tailor. A teacher. Yes. Yes.

A child.

Yes.

Over a period of 23 days, Aristides de Sousa Mendes rescued many thousands of people, including the painter Salvador Dalí; the writers Margret Rey and H. A. Rey; the entire Belgian cabinet; professors of medicine, biology, and physics who would go on to teach in America; and thousands of others whose lives are less known but no less precious.

Records are scarce, but it may have been the greatest individual act of rescue in all of World War II.

Author's Note

Aristides de Sousa Mendes was born on July 19, 1885, shortly after midnight. His twin brother, César, was born just before. Aristides grew up to study law, after which he began his career as a diplomat, traveling the world. Aristides and his wife raised 14 children, including two who died in 1934. The Sousa Mendes family lived in their Portuguese home, a country estate called Casa do Passal, in the town of Cabanas de Viriato. It was here that the family spent vacations, holidays, and sometimes weekends. Aristides would travel back and forth by train or car from wherever he was stationed. He even had a special car designed to transport his large family.

When Aristides was home at Casa do Passal, he greeted the village children with chocolate coins and sweets at holiday time. Aristides would often stand in front of the large kitchen oven, helping to bake and serve bread and soup on "the day of the poor," when the Casa do Passal kitchen would be left open for the needy people of the village to warm themselves and eat. Even when Aristides was abroad attending to his diplomatic duties, Casa do Passal's house manager would leave the kitchen door open.

In 1932, António de Oliveira Salazar was appointed prime minister of Portugal, and in 1938, he assigned Aristides to the position of consul general of Bordeaux, France. In November 1939, Prime Minister Salazar issued Circular 14—a memo that prevented Jewish people and other refugees from receiving passports or visas to Portugal without first securing permission from the Foreign Ministry.

Aristides asked the Foreign Ministry for permission to grant visas to Jewish people and other refugees many times, but he was either denied or given no reply. He disobeyed the prime minister, and from January 1, 1940, into June of 1940, Aristides granted visas to small groups escaping the war.

Aristides made nightly rounds in Bordeaux, during which he checked on the growing numbers of refugees. He met Rabbi Chaim Kruger, who had fled Brussels with his family and was helping other Jewish refugees stranded in Bordeaux. Rabbi Kruger would eventually become his friend. Aristides

promised the rabbi and his family visas and shelter in his apartment, but the rabbi declined. In Rabbi Kruger's 1967 deposition to Yad Vashem concerning the righteous deeds of Aristides, he said he insisted that Aristides help *all* the Jewish people who were stranded in Bordeaux before he would accept his friend's kind offer: "There was only one avenue of rescue—to give all of us visas to Portugal."

(The rabbi and his family were among those Aristides helped escort to the border gate after the bridge between France and Spain was closed. Aristides met Rabbi Kruger again in Lisbon, where they both were being helped by the Jewish aid societies there. They hugged each other happily. Rabbi Kruger and his family eventually sailed to America in 1941.)

Once the Nazis invaded France, many thousands of refugees tried to flee to Portugal. Aristides faced a moral dilemma—should he help the refugees and risk hurting his family, himself, and his career? After three days and nights of solitary contemplation and struggling within himself, on June 16, 1940, he embarked on what became "perhaps the largest rescue action by a single individual during the Holocaust."

Aristides received help from others in issuing these thousands of visas: his family; his consular secretary in Bordeaux, José de Seabra; Rabbi Chaim Kruger, who helped deliver visas in Bordeaux; Manuel de Vieira Braga, who was the consular secretary in Bayonne; and Emile Gissot, the vice-consul in Toulouse whom Aristides called and asked to issue approximately 10,000 visas to refugees trapped there. Even if people did not possess the necessary official paperwork, Aristides signed and stamped any piece of paper, even newspapers, to save as many families as possible.

On June 26, 1940, after helping the refugees in Hendaye, Aristides returned to Bordeaux. By this time, Prime Minister Salazar had already ordered him to return to Portugal, but Aristides still tried to save as many people as he could. He forged Portuguese passports for any Jewish people still stranded in Bordeaux. A Portuguese passport would help prevent them from being sent to concentration camps. On June 27, German soldiers entered

Bordeaux, and on the following day, they reached Hendaye.

On July 8, 1940, Aristides returned to Portugal. He was arrested, was taken to Lisbon by the secret police, and stood trial. He was stripped of his job and diplomatic title, and he and his children were prevented from working or attending universities in Portugal for the rest of their lives. Aristides also lost his beloved Casa do Passal, which was seized by the bank and eventually sold to pay his debts.

Aristides had to feed his wife and children in soup kitchens and with the assistance of other aid societies led by the Jewish community in Lisbon. Isaac Bitton, who helped in one of those soup kitchens, recalled the day he saw Aristides enter with his family:

> One day I heard a voice behind me speaking perfect Portuguese. I turned round and saw a man wearing a black suit and a diplomat's hat. Impressed by his presence, I went up to him and told him that next to the dining-room for refugees there was another room, on the left, for the Portuguese. He looked at me with a strange smile and said in a very calm voice: "You know, we are all refugees."

In those early days of World War II, long before the horrors of the Holocaust were fully realized, Aristides provided safe passage to Portugal for thousands of refugees. Aristides never thought of himself as a hero. He always believed his decision to help the refugees was the right one, and he wished he could have done more. "I could not have acted otherwise," he said, "and I therefore accept all that has befallen me with love."

Before he died in 1954, Aristides "asked his children to clear his name and have the honor of the family restored." Their work has spanned decades. After many years, his deeds began to be recognized. According to the Sousa Mendes Foundation, "The first recognition came in 1966 from Israel, which declared Aristides de

Sousa Mendes to be 'Righteous among the Nations.'" The honor came in the form of a medal given to non-Jewish people who took great risks to save Jewish people during the Holocaust. The US Congress issued a declaration to honor Aristides' bravery in 1986, and then in 1987 to 1988, Portuguese president Mário Soares "apologized to the Sousa Mendes family and the Portuguese Parliament promoted him posthumously to the rank of Ambassador." In 2017, Gerald Mendes, one of Aristides' grandsons, accepted the Grand Cross of the Order of Liberty—Portugal's highest honor—on his grandfather's behalf. It was presented by Portugal's current president, Marcelo Rebelo de Sousa. "There are no homage and posthumous decorations that give back all the life destroyed, all the injustice committed, all persecution inexorably maintained," the president said. "There are never complete reparations, but there are acknowledgments of guilt, there are exemplary evocations for the past, urgent warnings for the present, inevitable lessons for the future."

"He who saves a single life, saves the world entire."

—Talmud

Timeline

23 Days in 1940—Aristides de Sousa Mendes' Heroic Rescue

June 16, 1940: After three days of seclusion when, sick with worry, he pondered how to help the refugees, Aristides declares: "From now on, I will give visas to everyone." He sets up a production line in his Bordeaux consulate and begins signing visas for any refugee families who need them. Paul Reynaud steps down as French prime minister, admitting France's defeat by the Nazis.

June 17–19, 1940: Thousands of refugees stranded in Bordeaux hear that Aristides is giving out visas and arrive at the consulate. Aristides and others sign and stamp visas, day and night.

June 19, 1940: The Luftwaffe (the aerial warfare branch of the German Wehrmacht military forces) bombs Bordeaux, killing more than 80 people, wounding over 100 others, and damaging the city. Thousands of refugees flee to Bayonne and Hendaye, France.

June 20, 1940: The refugee crowds slow due to the bombing. Aristides continues to give visas to any remaining families. He orders Emile Gissot (vice-consul in Toulouse) to give visas to 10,000 refugees there. Aristides drives along the crowded road to Bayonne, where thousands more refugees need visas. He creates another visa production line, this time in the street, aided by the consular secretary in Bayonne, Manuel de Vieira Braga. The consul of Bayonne, Faria Machado, reports Aristides' disobedience to the new prime minister, António de Oliveira Salazar. The British embassy in Lisbon condemns Aristides and his "irregularities" in visa-signing, and reports this to the Foreign Ministry. Prime Minister Salazar begins the process of stopping Aristides' actions.

June 21, 1940: Portugal's Foreign Ministry sends an aide, Armando Lopo Simeão, to investigate whether the reports about Aristides' disobedience are true.

June 21–22, 1940: Aristides continues signing visas in Bayonne. Prime Minister Salazar orders Aristides' arrest.

June 23, 1940: Prime Minister Salazar sends a telegram to Aristides in Bordeaux, announcing that he has taken away Aristides' right to issue visas. Consequently, Aristides loses his authority. But he is now in Hendaye, still saving as many lives as he can, and will not receive the telegram until he returns to Bordeaux.

June 23–25, 1940: While in Hendaye, Aristides meets with the Portuguese ambassador to Spain and Prime Minister Salazar's friend, Pedro Teotónio Pereira, who tells Aristides: "Orders must be obeyed." Aristides responds: "Not if those orders are incompatible with human feeling." Aristides tries to help refugees at the border of Hendaye and Irún, Spain, when the bridge linking both countries, Freedom Bridge, is sealed on June 24, 1940. Prime Minister Salazar orders Aristides to return to Portugal immediately. Pereira, under authority of the prime minister, declares that refugees holding visas signed by Aristides de Sousa Mendes in Bordeaux and Bayonne are forbidden to pass. Pereira does not want to anger the Spanish government with the large numbers of refugees who want to enter Spain to travel to Portugal. Aristides escorts some refugees to an isolated border post with no telephone, hoping the guards have not received Prime Minister Salazar's orders. The guards permit the refugees to cross into Spain.

June 26–July 8, 1940: Aristides is back in Bordeaux. Since he has lost his consular authority, he begins forging Portuguese passports for stranded Jewish people and other refugees to prevent them from being sent to concentration camps. A Portuguese passport helps guarantee their safety.

June 27, 1940: The German army enters Bordeaux.

July 4, 1940: Prime Minister Salazar orders the opening of disciplinary proceedings against Aristides.

July 8, 1940: Aristides and his wife return to Portugal.

Quotes and Sources

"It is not just my family who needs help, but all my fellow Jews who are in danger for their lives." Chaim Kruger, in José-Alain Fralon, *A Good Man in Evil Times: The Story of Aristides de Sousa Mendes—The Man Who Saved the Lives of Countless Refugees in World War II*, trans. Peter Graham (New York: Carroll and Graf, 2000), 57.

"From now on, I will give visas to everyone." Aristides de Sousa Mendes, in José-Alain Fralon, *Aristides de Sousa Mendes: Le Juste de Bordeaux* (1998; repr., Bordeaux, France: Bouquins/Mollat, 2024), 72. Author's translation.

"Next person, please." Aristides de Sousa Mendes, in Fralon, *A Good Man in Evil Times*, 66.

"Quick, hide that in your pocket." Aristides de Sousa Mendes, in Fralon, *A Good Man in Evil Times*, 63.

"I am the Portuguese consul. These people are with me." Aristides de Sousa Mendes, in Mordecai Paldiel, *Diplomat Heroes of the Holocaust* (Jersey City, NJ: KTAV, 2007), 79.

"It was indeed my aim to 'save all those people,' whose suffering was indescribable." Aristides de Sousa Mendes, in Manuela Franco, ed., *Spared Lives: The Actions of Three Portuguese Diplomats in World War II*, trans. Alexandra Andresen Leitao (Lisbon, Portugal: Ministry of Foreign Affairs, 2000), 79; and Paldiel, *Diplomat Heroes of the Holocaust*, 82.

"There was only one avenue of rescue—to give all of us visas to Portugal." Chaim Kruger, in Paldiel, *Diplomat Heroes of the Holocaust*, 74.

"Perhaps the largest rescue action by a single individual during the Holocaust." Yehuda Bauer, Holocaust historian, in Sousa Mendes Foundation, "Aristides de Sousa Mendes: His Life and Legacy," accessed February 17, 2023, https://sousamendesfoundation.org/aristides-de-sousa-mendes-his-life-and-legacy/.

"One day I heard a voice behind me speaking perfect Portuguese. I turned round and saw a man wearing a black suit and a diplomat's hat. Impressed by his presence, I went up to him and told him that next to the dining-room for refugees there was another room, on the left, for the Portuguese. He looked at me with a strange smile and said in a very calm voice: 'You know, we are all refugees.'" Isaac Bitton, in Fralon, *A Good Man in Evil Times*, 119.

"I could not have acted otherwise, and I therefore accept all that has befallen me with love." Aristides de Sousa Mendes, in Sousa Mendes Foundation, "Aristides de Sousa Mendes: His Life and Legacy."

"[He] asked his children to clear his name and have the honor of the family restored." Sousa Mendes Foundation, "Aristides de Sousa Mendes: His Life and Legacy."

"The first recognition came in 1966 from Israel, which declared Aristides de Sousa Mendes to be 'Righteous among the Nations.'" Sousa Mendes Foundation, "Aristides de Sousa Mendes: His Life and Legacy."

"President Mario Soares apologized to the Sousa Mendes family and the Portuguese Parliament promoted him posthumously to the rank of Ambassador." Sousa Mendes Foundation, "Aristides de Sousa Mendes: His Life and Legacy."

"'There are no homage and posthumous decorations that give back all the life destroyed, all the injustice committed, all persecution inexorably maintained. . . . There are never complete reparations, but there are acknowledgments of guilt, there are exemplary evocations for the past, urgent warnings for the present, inevitable lessons for the future.'" Marcelo Rebelo de Sousa, in Sousa Mendes Foundation, "Posthumous Honor for Sousa Mendes," April 3, 2017, https://sousamendesfoundation.org/posthumous-honor-for-sousa-mendes/.

"Orders must be obeyed." Pedro Teotónio Pereira, in Paldiel, *Diplomat Heroes of the Holocaust*, 80.

"Not if those orders are incompatible with human feeling." Aristides de Sousa Mendes, in Paldiel, *Diplomat Heroes of the Holocaust*, 80.

Bibliography

Primary Sources

Bagger, Eugene. "Testimonial of Eugene Bagger" (n.d.). Sousa Mendes Foundation. Accessed February 17, 2023. http://sousamendesfoundation.org/family/bagger.

Birnbaum, Daniel. "Testimonial of Daniel Birnbaum" (1942). Sousa Mendes Foundation. Accessed February 17, 2023. http://sousamendesfoundation.org/family/birnbaum.

Bromberger, Sylvain. "Testimonial of Sylvain Bromberger" (1999). Sousa Mendes Foundation. Accessed February 17, 2023. http://sousamendesfoundation.org/family/bromberger.

Jay, Marcelle. "Testimonial of Marcelle Jay Née Byre" (November 2012). Sousa Mendes Foundation. Accessed February 17, 2023. http://sousamendesfoundation.org/family/byre.

Krieger, Haim [Chaim Kruger]. "Testimony of Rabbi Haim Krieger" (1966). Dossier Aristides Sousa Mendes, M31/264. Yad

Vashem Archives, Jerusalem. Excerpt: https://www.yadvashem.org/righteous/stories/mendes/krieger-testimony.html.

Kruger, Chaim. "Testimonial of Rabbi Chaim Kruger" (August 8, 1941). Sousa Mendes Foundation. Accessed February 17, 2023. http://sousamendesfoundation.org/family/kruger.

Mendes, César. "Testimony of César Mendes" (n.d.). Dossier Aristides Sousa Mendes, M31/264. Yad Vashem Archives, Jerusalem. Excerpt: https://www.yadvashem.org/righteous/stories/mendes/mendes-testimony.html.

Oesterreicher, Harry. Telephone interview. May 22, 2014.

Rollin, Marguerite. "Testimonial of Marguerite Rollin Née Galimir" (March 4, 1966). Sousa Mendes Foundation. Accessed February 17, 2023. http://sousamendesfoundation.org/family/galimir.

Smolar, Boris. "Testimonial of Boris Smolar" (June 27, 1940). Sousa Mendes Foundation. Accessed February 17, 2023. http://sousamendesfoundation.org/family/smolar.

Sousa Mendes Foundation. "Ruth Charchat and Georgette Standish Interview." October 10, 2013. Video, 27:05 min. https://www.youtube.com/watch?v=YnvdLHl5yFU.

Secondary Sources

Borden, Louise. *The Journey That Saved Curious George: The True Wartime Escape of Margret and H. A. Rey*. Boston: Houghton Mifflin, 2005.

Fogelman, Eva. *Conscience and Courage: Rescuers of Jews during the Holocaust*. New York: Anchor Books, 1994.

Fontoura, Priscilla, dir. *I Am Alive Thanks to Aristides de Sousa Mendes*. Porto, Portugal: Lula Gigante Productions, 2013. DVD, 24:32 min.

Fralon, José-Alain. *A Good Man in Evil Times: The Story of Aristides de Sousa Mendes—The Man Who Saved the Lives of Countless Refugees in World War II*. Translated by Peter Graham. New York: Carroll and Graf, 2000.

Franco, Manuela, ed. *Spared Lives: The Actions of Three Portuguese Diplomats in World War II*. Translated by Alexandra Andresen Leitao. Lisbon, Portugal: Ministry of Foreign Affairs, 2000.

History Channel. *Diplomats for the Damned*. Aired 2000. New York: A&E Television Networks, 2008. DVD, 50 min.

House, Christian. "Sousa Mendes Saved More Lives than Schindler So Why Isn't He a Household Name Too?" *The Independent*, October 17, 2010. https://www.independent.co.uk/news/people/profiles/sousa-mendes-saved-more-lives-than-schindler-so-why-isn-t-he-a-household-name-too-2105882.html.

Jewish Foundation for the Righteous, The. "Aristides de Sousa Mendes, France." Stories of Rescue. Accessed February 17, 2023. https://jfr.org/rescuer-stories/sousa-mendes-aristides-de/.

Kristof, Nicholas. "Would You Hide a Jew from the Nazis?" *The New York Times*, September 17, 2016. https://www.nytimes.com/2016/09/18/opinion/sunday/would-you-hide-a-jew-from-the-nazis.html.

Manso, Francisco, and João Côrrea, dir. *The Consul of Bordeaux—Aristides de Sousa Mendes*. Lisbon, Portugal: Take 2000, 2011. DVD, 90 min.

Mendes, Louis-Philippe. "Holocaust Remembrance Day: Honoring a Rescuer Who Saved 30,000 People." *Huffington Post*, April 18, 2012, updated June 19, 2012. https://www.huffpost.com/entry/holocaust-remembrance-day_b_1434733.

Minder, Raphael. "In Portugal, a Protector of a People Is Honored." *The New York Times*, July 9, 2013. https://www.nytimes.com/2013/07/10/world/europe/in-portugal-a-protector-of-a-people-is-honored.html.

Olga, Teresa, dir. *Aristides de Sousa Mendes: O Cônsul Injustiçado*. Lisbon, Portugal: Rádio e Televisão de Portugal, 1992. DVD, 60 min.

Paldiel, Mordecai. *Diplomat Heroes of the Holocaust*. Jersey City, NJ: KTAV, 2007.

——. *The Righteous among the Nations: Rescuers of Jews during the Holocaust*. Jerusalem: Yad Vashem; New York: HarperCollins, 2007.

Pinkhasov, Semyon, dir. *With God against Man*. 2016. Video, 46:29 min. https://tubitv.com/movies/341562/with-god-against-man.

Santoni, Joël, dir. *Disobedience: The Sousa Mendes Story*. Paris: Panama Productions, 2009. DVD, 103 min.

Schiffman, Lisa. "Diplomat Who Saved Jews Gains Recognition." *Newsday*, November 29, 2012. https://www.newsday.com/beta/lifestyle/retirement/diplomat-who-saved-jews-gains-recognition-f47893.

Yad Vashem. "Aristides de Sousa Mendes." The Righteous among the Nations: Featured Stories. Accessed February 17, 2023. https://www.yadvashem.org/righteous/stories/mendes.html.

INK